The Alphabet of Music

The Alphabet of Music

By ROBERT W. SURPLUS

Illustrated by GEORGE OVERLIE

Musical Books for Young People

LERNER PUBLICATIONS COMPANY
MINNEAPOLIS, MINNESOTA

To Amy and Melanie

International Copyright Secured. Printed in U.S.A.

Library of Congress Catalog Card Number: 62-20799

Third Printing 1964

CONTENTS

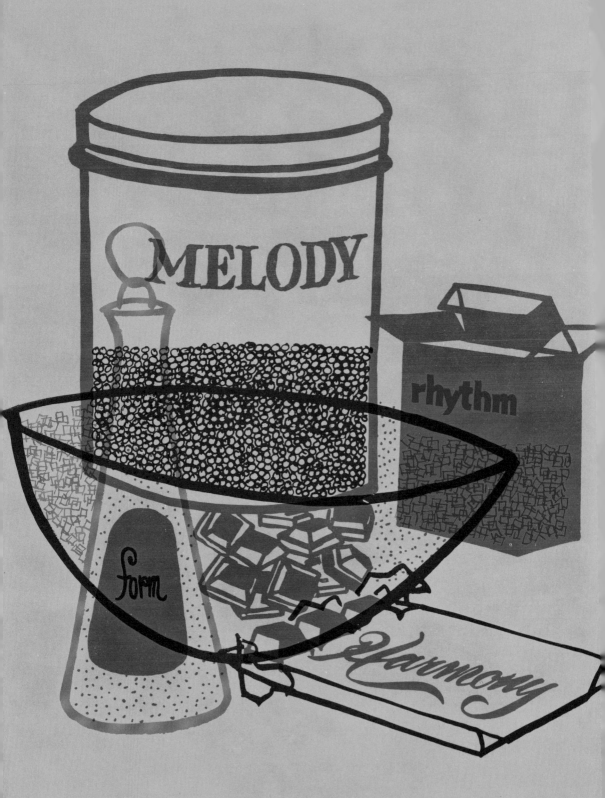

DO YOU KNOW THE INGREDIENTS OF MUSIC?

Have you ever thought about how many times a day you hear music? Can you think of the many different kinds of music it is possible to hear during a day? You might hear a folk tune or a symphony; a rock-and-roll singer or an opera tenor; a square-dance band or a string quartet; a singing commercial or a fine choir; a stirring march or a church hymn. You have probably heard all these kinds of music at sometime.

Have you ever watched mom as she made some "brownies" for you and a chocolate cake for dad? The *ingredients,* or the things she puts into them, are much the same, but the amounts of each ingredient used are different.

During the day, you are sure to listen to many people talk. The words we use are called language. They are made up of 26 letters called the alphabet. No matter what kind of speaking or reading is done, these letters are a part of the words used. But the ideas that come from these same 26 letters can be very different. Much depends upon how they are put together.

As the ingredients in "brownies" and chocolate cake are the same, and as the same twenty-six letters of the alphabet are used for all reading or speaking, so also are the "musical ingredients" the same for all the kinds of music mentioned above. A symphony may sound far different from a folk tune, a march far different from a hymn, and a singing commercial far different from a fine choir, but they all use the same ingredients.

Do you know what these ingredients are? This book will tell you what they are and how they are used to make music.

MELODY

Perhaps the easiest ingredient of music for us to recognize is the *melody,* or tune. When you think of a piece of music, you remember the melody.

Some kinds of music are made up of just melody. Many folk songs, chants, and old church music called *plainsong* are examples of music that is just melody.

What is melody? We remember it easily, and we call it the tune, but how do we explain it to someone else? We might say that melody is a group of sounds arranged in a way that is pleasing to our ears. Sometimes it is hard to say what is pleasing, since some of us like one kind of melody, while others like another kind. Certainly, the composers of today write music with melodies far different from the music of one-hundred years ago.

EXAMPLE 1

Notice the melodies written below. If you can play the piano or another instrument, play these melodies to find out how they sound. If you don't play an instrument, maybe you have learned enough about reading music to hum or sing the tune. Perhaps, in your school, you guess the names of mystery tunes and have had practice at telling what a song is by looking at the notes of the melody.

EXAMPLE 2

HOT CROSS BUNS

Hot cross buns, Hot cross buns, One a pen - ny, Two a pen - ny, Hot cross buns.

EXAMPLE 3

POP! GOES THE WEASEL

All a - round the mul - ber - ry bush, The mon - key chased the wea - sel, The

mon - key thought 'twas all — in fun. Pop! goes the weas - el.

EXAMPLE 4

ALL THROUGH THE NIGHT

Sleep my child and peace at -tend thee All through the night; Guard -ian an -gels God will send thee All through the night,

Soft the drow -sy hours are creep-ing, Hill and vale in slum-ber steep-ing, I my lov -ing vi -gil keep-ing All through the night.

After you sing or play the three examples given, the music will stay in your mind. These are easy songs to remember, and you will know them when you hear them again. Using your memory, think over the tune of each song. Can you show, by raising or lowering your hand, how the music goes? If you can, you are making a picture of the melody. You can check how well you do this by looking at the music at the same time you make the picture of the melody.

You probably noticed that example 2 did not require you to move your hand around too much. In fact, each note of the melody was only one note away from the note before or after it. We say that such a melody moves in *steps,* since it doesn't jump around. A melody like this is easier to sing than one that jumps around.

Now, let's think about example 3. Try showing the picture of this music as you recall the melody. Your hand has to jump around a lot to do this one correctly. Now, look at the music. You can also see that the notes jump around.

A minute ago, when you were using your hand to picture the music from memory, you were also using your ear. When you use your eyes to help your ears with the melody, you are then reading music.

Let's try the same thing on example 4. Notice that this music is like example 2—it moves mostly in steps. Melodies that move in steps are usually smoother and quieter than melodies that move in skips. They are often very restful, while a melody that moves in skips usually makes you want to run, jump, skip, or tap your feet in time to the music.

There is a difference between melodies written for voices and those written for instruments. While it is not always easy to play skips on an instrument, it is easier than singing big skips. On an instrument there are keys and your fingers to help you find the notes, but when singing, you must depend on your ears alone.

The number of notes that can be performed, or the *range,* is also different for voices and instruments. You will find that most music for voices has a range of about an *octave,* or eight notes. It is possible to write music with a bigger range for instruments, especially for the piano and the stringed instruments.

Most of the melodies you hear will be built around two things: scales and chords. Let's find out how.

Today, almost everyone knows what a scale is, but in case you've forgotten, let's refresh your memory. Scales have been used for centuries. Before anyone took the trouble to arrange notes in the special order we call scales, people sang music that followed certain scale patterns. They may not have known that their music followed the same order over and over, but it really did. The Chinese and the Greeks finally decided upon the order of the notes in scales. Once the pattern for scales was decided upon, scales became an important part of all music.

What does a scale look like? You have certainly climbed stairs. You know that you start at the bottom, and by taking a step at a time, you reach the top. Scales are like stairs. If you start playing at the bottom note and play each note in the scale, you will get to the top.

This is what a C-scale looks like.

Notice how the notes go up, one at a time, to reach the top. Without the staff you could imagine steps something like this.

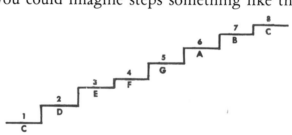

Notice the numbers over the stairs. This is to show you that there are eight notes in a scale. A scale could also be shown this way.

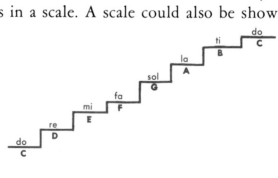

A scale, then, is like a stairway of eight notes in alphabetical order. If you play eight notes, going up one note at a time so that the eighth note is an octave above the first note, you have a scale.

Maybe, some of you remember playing step-bells in school. Step-bells look exactly like a flight of stairs, and when you play each note from bottom to top you play a scale.

There is one big difference between a scale and a flight of stairs. If stairs have been made correctly, all the steps will be the same height. But in a scale, some steps are smaller than others. We call the smaller steps *half-steps,* and the larger ones *whole-steps.*

How we place half-steps and whole-steps in a scale pattern tells the kind of scale we get. Here is the pattern for a major scale.

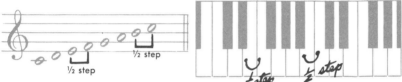

All the steps are whole-steps except E to F, and B to C. Notice how there are half-steps between the third and fourth and seventh and eighth notes. No matter what major scale is written you will find the half-steps in the same place. Notice the following examples.

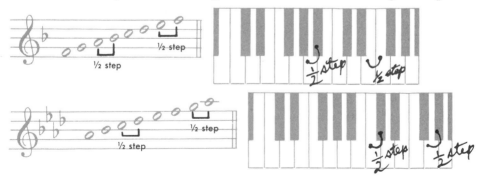

Look at the pattern for a minor scale.

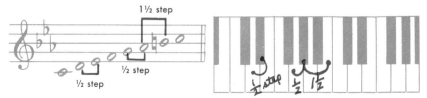

The above scale is called a *harmonic minor* scale. No matter where a harmonic minor scale is started you will find a half-step between the second and third notes, the fifth and sixth notes and the seventh and eighth notes. You will also find 1½-steps between the sixth and seventh notes. Here is another harmonic minor scale. See if this is true.

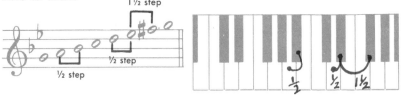

Most of the songs you know in minor key are probably in harmonic minor scale, but you may have sung a *natural minor* scale such as this one,

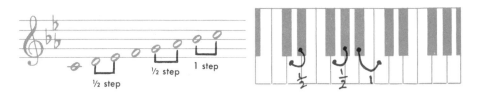

or a *melodic minor* scale like this one.

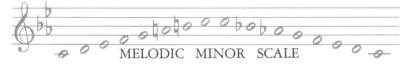

MELODIC MINOR SCALE

Notice that a melodic minor scale uses different notes going up than coming down. The other minor scales are the same, whether going up or down.

Try each of these scales on an instrument and notice how they are different. The slightest difference means a lot in music. Just changing a note in a melody one half-step changes the sound completely. Here is a well-known melody in major key. Then just below it is the same melody in a minor key. Play or sing both examples. Notice how different they sound.

HOT CROSS BUNS (Major Key)

(Minor Key)

Another kind of scale that is important is the *chromatic scale.* A chromatic scale is made up of all half-steps. Going up, it is written in sharps, while coming down, flats are used.

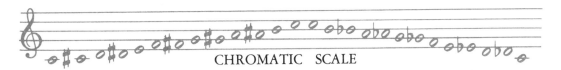

CHROMATIC SCALE

Scales are like families. All the notes are related to each other, but some are closer than others. The fourth note of the scale, *fa,* always wants to go down to be with the third note, *mi,* while the seventh note, *ti,* always wants to go up to *do.*

13

The most important note gives the scale its name. If *do* is on C, the scale is the C-scale. Most songs end on *do,* or as it is called, the *tonic.* When a melody comes back to *do* to end, it's like you and your family coming back home after a trip.

Scales are important because they act as a map, or guide, for melodies. A melody could move far away from known patterns if composers did not have scales as guides. If a melody does roam away from a known pattern, the listener always feels more content when it returns home to the scale or key from which it started.

Most melodies that jump around are built on chords. Chords are built on different tones of the scale. We can build a chord on each tone of the scale. We number them from one to seven to fit the notes of the scale upon which they are built.

I   ii   iii   IV   V   vi   vii°   I

Notice that the chords built on the first, fourth, and fifth notes of the scale are marked with large Roman numerals, while the others are given small numerals. The chords with large numerals beneath are major chords. The chords with small numerals are *minor chords,* except for the one built on the seventh note of the scale, which is a *diminished chord.*

Play the major chords on the piano. Hear how they sound. Then try the minor chords. The sound from these is different, isn't it? If someone were to play the chords while you had your eyes shut, could you tell which ones were major and which were minor?

14

Three chords are used more than the others. They are the I-chord, the IV-chord and the V_7-chord—the V chord with an extra note added to make it sound fuller. Here are these chords in the key of F. Notice how they are built on the *first,* the *fourth,* and the *fifth* notes of the scale.

Here is the V_7-chord written an octave lower.

Can you find the notes of this chord in *Ten Little Indians?* Notice how this song which you learned when you were small is built almost entirely on notes from the I and V_7-chords.

TEN LITTLE INDIANS

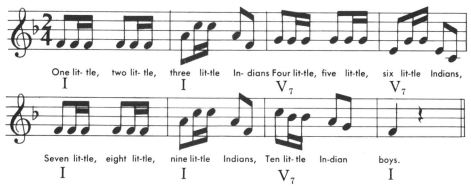

As most songs end on *do* or the tonic of the scale, so also do most songs end on the *do* or I-chord. Music has a finished sound when it returns home to the I-chord.

All melodies have a shape, or picture. When people learn to read music they follow the "picture of the melody" to see how the music goes. Some melodies go up like the one below.

BEETHOVEN - FIRST SYMPHONY

Here is an example that goes down the scale. Can you name the tune?

Another kind of melody moves up and down around one tone. Its picture would look like this.

RIMSKY- KORSAKOFF- SCHEHERAZADE

16

Still another kind of melody is shaped like a rainbow.

DVORAK - NEW WORLD SYMPHONY

A melody whose picture is the opposite of the last melody would be shaped like a bowl.

HANDEL - JOY TO THE WORLD

Try listening to some songs you like and then draw the picture of each song's melody. You'll be surprised at how much this helps in understanding music.

17

RHYTHM

When man first made music, he probably started by beating sticks together or by hitting a hollow log with a stick. This, of course, was just rhythm, without melody. Of the ingredients that go together to make up music, rhythm then, is the oldest.

What exactly is rhythm? In music, the word rhythm means the steady beat of time. It refers to time patterns that repeat over and over again. Some people have the idea that only fast music has rhythm. This is not so. Rhythm is found in all music, whether it is slow or fast. When we hear slow music we listen to a slow, steady flow of music in time. When we hear quick, lively music we also hear rhythm, but at a much faster *tempo,* or speed.

When dad drives the car he watches the speedometer to know how fast he's going. Also, signs are found along the way to tell him the speed limit. In music, the conductor tells us how fast to go. We also have a music speedometer, called a *metronome,* to help out. In addition, we find signs to tell us how fast to go. Both conductors and musicians are used to these signs which they call *tempo signs.* They are usually written in Italian.

Some of the most common are:

Largo	—	very slow
Adagio	—	slow
Andante	—	moderately slow, at a walking tempo
Moderato	—	moderately
Allegretto	—	moderately fast.
Allegro	—	fast
Presto	—	very fast

Actually, rhythm is everywhere. When you run or play you are moving to a certain rhythm. Rhythm makes you want to tap your feet to music, or dance, or march. There is a rhythm to the way the sun rises each morning and sets each evening. There is rhythm in the way each day turns to night. The tides of the mighty ocean move to a definite rhythm, and so people know when to expect high or low tide. Your own body has a certain rhythm. As your heart beat is important to your life, so is rhythm important to music—it keeps it going.

Rhythm has a big effect on melody. Sometimes the rhythm is so "catchy" that you remember it more than the sound of the melody. Usually, however, people think of the rhythm and melody at the same time.

Here are some rhythm patterns from melodies you have heard. Try clapping these patterns. Can you tell what the melodies are? Remember, the long dashes get more time than the short ones.

The names of these songs will be found on page 41.

Have you ever paid much attention to a band as it marched down the street in a parade? Maybe you heard this rhythm which is standard for most bands.

$\frac{2}{4}$ ♩ ♪ ♪ | ♩ ♪ ♪ | ♩ ♩ | ♩ ♪ ♪ ‖

Whatever rhythm you heard, you probably tapped your foot in time to the music.

Why does a person tap his foot to music? Is this helpful in any way? People tap their feet on notes that are *accented,* or played slightly louder. Suppose you had a drum handy and could play these notes, making each note sound the same. ♩ ♩ ♩ ♩

Now play the same notes over and over again, but accent (play louder) the first and third notes as shown here: > > . The

little v-shaped sign turned on its side is an *accent sign.* Using accents makes the beat of a drum sound more interesting.

As music became more complicated, musicians needed something to make music reading easier. Finally, around 1620, music was divided up into *measures* by little lines call *bar-lines.* By this time, everyone was quite used to accents, and the bar-line was placed just before an accent.
A measure in 3/4 time would look like this $\frac{3}{4}$ ♩ ♩ ♩ . A measure

in 2/4 time would look like this $\frac{2}{4}$ ♩ ♩ |

and a measure in 4/4 time would look like this $\frac{4}{4}$ ♩ ♩ ♩ ♩ |

4/4 time usually requires two accents, one on the first beat and one on the third.

The signs 2/4, 3/4, and 4/4 show how many beats there are in a measure. For example, in the sign 2/4 the upper number tells that there will be two beats in a measure. The lower number tells that a quarter note will get one beat.

It is quite easy to sense what the *meter,* or time, of a piece of music is. As you listen, start to clap in time to the music. From the swing of the music, you will be able to tell whether the piece is in *duple* (2 beats) or *triple* (3 beats) time. You will soon discover that all music swings in 2's or 3's, or a combination of both.

You might be curious about the last statement. What about 4/4 time or 6/8 time? Well, 4/4 time would be duple rhythm since it would be made up of two 2's. And 6/8 time would either be duple if it were a fast march-type piece, or triple-time if it were a slow piece, since 6 would be made up of two 3's.

Even time signatures such as 5/4 are made up of 2's and 3's put together. Notice the examples below. The first one divides into a three-pattern and then a two-pattern, while the second example would have a two-pattern followed by a three-pattern.

While the accent usually comes on the first beat of a measure, there are times when it comes at another place. When a beat other than the regularly accented beat is emphasized, or when a strongly accented note comes between two regular beats, musicians say the music is *syncopated.* Syncopation is used a great deal in jazz, South American music, and Negro spirituals. Notice how the accent of the melody is not found on the beats that are usually accented.

Two ideas cover all the rhythmic patterns that can be made up. Patterns are made up of *even notes* such as

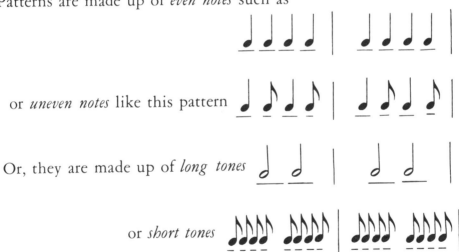

No matter what rhythms you may see, these two ideas —*long* and *short* and *even* and *uneven*—cover all rhythmic patterns.

23

Also, in every song you hear, there are at least three rhythms going on all the time. Suppose we find out what three rhythms are found in every song.

To do this, let's think of a tune you know very well. In the United States we call it *America,* while in England and Canada it is *God Save the Queen.*

AMERICA

We said earlier that most of the music you know swings in two's or three's. This means you can count ONE—two or ONE—two—three as you listen to, or play the music. If you clap ONE—two—three over and over again while you listen to *America* you are clapping the *rhythm of the beat.* This is the beat that holds music together. It stays exactly the same until the piece of music is finished.

Earlier we also mentioned how each melody has a rhythm pattern all its own. The rhythm pattern of any song is called the *rhythm of the melody.*

Each measure also has an accent. In 3/4 time, the time for *America*, it always comes on the first beat of the measure. Can you think of the tune for *America* but only clap on the first beat of each measure? If you can, you are clapping the accents.

Try to get some of your friends together to demonstrate how there is always more than one rhythm in a piece of music. If you were to see the three different parts in notes they would look like this. No pitches are shown in this example.

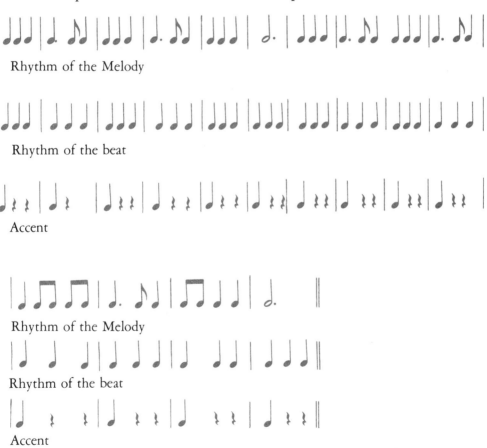

Rhythm of the Melody

Rhythm of the beat

Accent

Rhythm of the Melody

Rhythm of the beat

Accent

In order to understand music, you should be familiar with the different notes and rests that are used. You know that notes are used to show how high or low people are to sing or play. Since music is "sound in time", a system of differently shaped notes and rests helps us keep the rhythm the composer wants.

Here are the notes and rests we use the most.

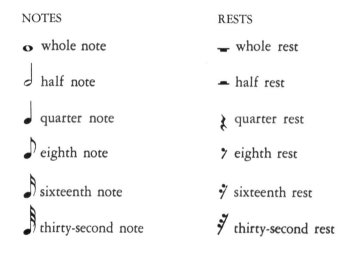

NOTES	RESTS
o whole note	▬ whole rest
♩ half note	▬ half rest
♩ quarter note	𝄽 quarter rest
♪ eighth note	𝄾 eighth rest
♬ sixteenth note	𝄿 sixteenth rest
♬ thirty-second note	𝅀 thirty-second rest

In a piece of music with the same tempo or speed all the way through, a whole note is always longer than a half, a half longer than a quarter, a quarter longer than an eighth, an eighth longer than a sixteenth, and a sixteenth longer than a thirty-second note.

This chart shows how some of these notes compare in length to whole notes.

Sometimes dots are used with notes and rests. A dot adds half the value to whatever note or rest that it follows.

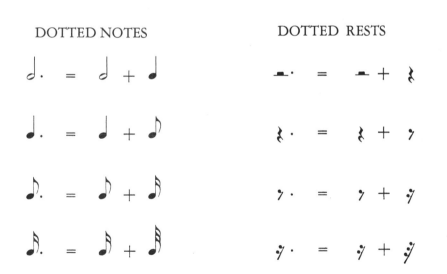

DOTTED NOTES

DOTTED RESTS

HARMONY

So far, we've talked about melody and rhythm. Now let's turn to another important part of music—*harmony*. The word harmony means a pleasing sound. When harmony notes are added to a melody you get a more pleasing sound, much richer and fuller than if you hear just melody alone.

When music first started, remember, it was just rhythm. Then for many, many years it was made up of rhythm and melody. This type of music, melody with rhythm, was called *monody* or *monophonic music*. Music of this kind is still heard today in the Gregorian chants of the Catholic Church.

Sometime later, a very simple kind of harmony was heard. It was quite a bit like the sound you hear when you listen to bagpipes. This simple kind of harmony had one note held under the melody.

This one note was called a *drone*. Here is a song you know with a drone written under the melody.

ROW, ROW, ROW YOUR BOAT

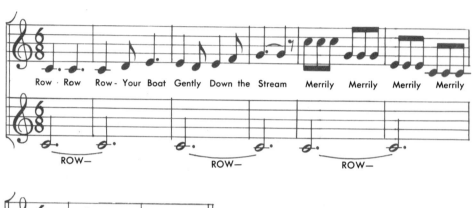

Also, a way of singing two or more melodies at once was started. Each of these melodies was a tune by itself, but they were all sung together to make a more interesting piece of music. Each part had different notes and a different rhythm from the other parts. This type of music with its many melodies was called *polyphony* (po-LIF-o-nee). It was not harmony as we know it today but was one of the steps toward harmony.

30

Polyphony is like a round. You have probably sung *Are You Sleeping* sometime during your days in school. Notice how the same melody looks when started at different times by different voices. It sounds much fuller and richer when sung this way.

ARE YOU SLEEPING ?

One of the first attempts at polyphony was the practice of having a second part four or five notes below the melody. Play the examples below on the piano and see how they sound to you.

To our ears today this type of music, called *organum*, does not sound pleasing, but centuries ago it was the newest kind of music.

In time, polyphonic music gave way to a newer kind, called *homophonic* (ho-mo-FAHN-ik) music. This music used a single melody at a time. *Chords*, or groups of notes which sounded good with a melody made up a background. This music is something like a picture and a frame — the melody is the picture, and the chords are the frame. The right frame can do a lot for a picture, the same as the right chord can make a melody sound more interesting.

We mentioned chords, or a group of tones played at the same time, when we showed how melodies are made. Remember, there are several kinds of chords.

First there are major chords like this one.

Then we have minor chords

diminished chords and augmented chords.

All these chords are used to make melodies sound more interesting. There are also other chords that are used to make harmony.

You may recognize some of the chords that are written above. If you don't, however, you may recognize 3rds and 6ths. These are harmony parts from songs you may have sung in school. Thirds look like this.

Sixths look like this.

Both 3rds and 6ths have a sweet, pleasant sound. They are used for harmony parts in many songs.

33

FORM

Now that we've talked about the materials that make up music let's turn to how these materials are put together. Musicians call this the *form* of music.

Everything that we do has a certain form. Your teacher runs a classroom to follow a certain form. Different teachers run classes in different ways, but there is some form that all teachers follow. When you go to church the ritual of your church follows a certain form. Every religion has form in its service. When, as a small child, you played hop-scotch, the game was laid out in a special form you followed. When boys play baseball, they follow a special form both in the playing field and in the number of outs each inning. No matter what we do, there is some kind of form or pattern to it.

Have you ever looked at a picture by a famous artist? If you have, you will notice that all the parts of the picture go together to make one *complete idea.* You will also see that there is *balance* between the different parts of the picture. Also, the artist will try to have *variety* in his picture—not everything will be the same and so there will be *contrasts.* Even if he has these things just mentioned, the artist will make sure that there is one idea that stands out above all the rest. We call this the *climax,* or the most important part of the picture.

Let's take a look at a very famous building. The Capitol Building in Washington, D. C., is a good example of what we want to show. Here we find balance, contrast, and climax shown very clearly. If we were giving letters to the parts of the Capitol we could say that the wing on the left is A, the middle part with the dome, B, and the wing on the right would be A, also, since it is the same as the other wing. There is form to this building.

This is A.   This is B.   This is A.

Can we find form in music? Let's look at a familiar tune to find out.

TWINKLE, TWINKLE LITTLE STAR

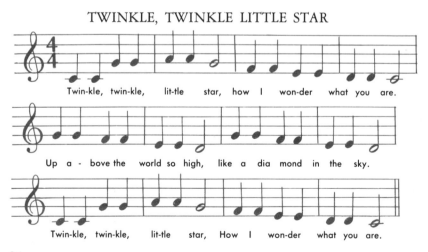

Twin-kle, twin-kle,   lit-tle   star, how I   won-der   what you   are.

Up a - bove the   world so high,   like a   dia mond in the   sky.

Twin-kle, twin-kle,   lit-tle   star, How I   won-der   what you   are.

We can tell that the first and third lines are alike, while the middle line is different. The first and third lines are *A* like the wings of the Capitol, while the second line is *B* like the dome section. B *contrasts* with the A parts and gives the music *variety.*

When you look at a picture, or see a building, your eye allows you to see the form, but in music you must use your memory unless you have the music in front of you. Also, you must remember the entire piece to be able to appreciate the form.

The form helps give the sense to a song. It makes the song easier to remember. The form of *Twinkle, Twinkle Little Star* is *ABA* form, or *Three-part-form.* It is found in many, many songs of all kinds.

Two-part-form or *AB* form has only two different parts to it, instead of two parts that are alike and one that is different. Here is a song in two-part-form.

GO TELL AUNT RHODIE

Go tell Aunt Rho - die, Go tell Aunt Rho - die,

Go tell Aunt Rho - die, The old grey goose is dead.

Another form that is quite easy to follow is called *rondo form.* One kind of rondo form is A B A B A, while another is A B A C A.

If you can understand two-part form and three-part form, then you will have a good start in understanding longer pieces of music. Most longer pieces divide into large sections of two or three parts.

MAKING UP A TUNE

Suppose a person started to compose a simple piece of music. Maybe, he was walking down the street when he had a musical idea he felt he wanted to write down. Or, he may have been sitting at the piano playing whatever notes came into his head.

Let's imagine he started with this musical idea.

Musicians call this little tiny section of music a *motive*. Whenever a person writes music he usually starts with a short tiny musical thought or motive. Do not think that this always happens quickly. Remember that music includes melody and rhythm, as well as form and harmony. Some people hear only rhythm and melody in their early thoughts, while others hear melody, rhythm, and harmony, while thinking about the form of the music at the same time.

So far all we have is one tiny musical idea. Let's see what is added to it to make a *phrase,* or a complete idea. A motive is not complete by itself. It needs more music to make it complete. By adding two measures so our tune is now like this, we have completed the phrase. You can always tell where a phrase ends, since the music breathes at that point. If you were singing words you would breathe at the end of a phrase.

We have said that contrast is important in music. When our friend adds another phrase it is different from the one just finished, and so we say it *contrasts,* or adds *variety.* The second phrase is like this.

Now, in order to make this sound complete, we must add some more music. Remember, earlier we told how music, in order to sound finished, usually ends on *do* or the key note of the scale. Let's see how the composer finishes his piece. Here is the last phrase.

Notice how the last line starts like the first, but the last two measures are different. The composer has changed them slightly so the music ends on *do.*

Now we have melody, rhythm and form. The form is ABA. The next step is to add harmony. Let's look at the complete piece with chords added to make it complete.

This is just a simple little piece, and it has been harmonized in a very easy style. Notice the top line, or melody. It has melody, or tune, plus rhythm. Notice the form. It is ABA or three-part form. And finally, notice the harmony or chords that make the music sound richer and fuller.

THE ALPHABET OF MUSIC

We have taken a look at melody, rhythm, harmony, and form, the ingredients of music. No matter what kind of music you hear, at least three of these ingredients will be present. In monophonic music, only harmony will be missing.

Whenever you listen to music think about these four ingredients. Your enjoyment of the music will be increased, if you understand more about its ingredients.

Twenty-six letters make up our alphabet. The different ways of putting these letters together give us our language.

Four main ingredients make up music. The different combinations of melody, rhythm, harmony, and form give us many different kinds of music. These four are the alphabet of music.

Answers to page 20: America, Jingle Bells, and Row, Row, Row Your Boat.

ABOUT THE AUTHOR

Robert W. Surplus, a native of Gouldsboro, Pennsylvania, has been active in music education almost twenty years. He has had experience in every phase of music education in the public schools, and has taught all age levels from kindergarten through graduate school. Formerly Supervisor of Music at Red Lion, Pennsylvania, Associate Professor at Shippensburg State College, Shippensburg, Pennsylvania, and Instructor at Teachers College, Columbia University, he is at present an Assistant Professor in the College of Education, University of Minnesota. A graduate of Susquehanna University with a Bachelor of Science degree and of Teachers College, Columbia with a Master of Arts degree, he is presently completing the requirements for a doctorate at Columbia University.